Amazing Real Life Mysteries

RAJIV JAYASWAL

INDIA • SINGAPORE • MALAYSIA

ISBN

Hardcase 979-8-89588-342-6
Paperback 979-8-89556-367-0

Index

Super Natural

Visions

Visions of Death

Introduction

Brain-of-God

This whole universe is a "BRAIN OF GOD". This brain can work at its hundred percent capacity. It can create Stars, Suns, Moons, and Galaxies. It can create anything or can destroy anything by just a thought and is not required to do anything manually.

Our brains are like the mini copy of God's brain. However, the main difference is that it can only do 8 to 9 percent of its total capacity. In modern history, only Einstein is believed to be able to use 13 percent of his brain's capacity.

Through Meditation, we can increase the capacity of our brains. Our brains are the centres of all our activities, desires, and thoughts. They control all our physical and mental activities. A person is considered alive as long as their brain works. A brain-dead person is considered dead.

Our thoughts, our desires, our passions, etc., engulf the brains completely, and they become like computers infected with viruses. Meditation is like an anti-virus to make our brains free from the web of desires, passions, and thoughts.

When the brain is calm, peaceful, and relaxed, its capacity increases. It becomes more concentrated and oriented toward the desired objectives of life. A person who meditates daily is calmer, more peaceful, and more goal-oriented compared to a person who never meditates.

There are certain portions in our brains which, if activated, can be instrumental in connecting our brains with the universal, omnipresent brain of God.

It was at that stage of MEDITATION that Yogis of the ancient period exclaimed in ecstasy, "Aham Braham ASMI" (I am God). So, spiritually, our brains can penetrate the universal brain of God through meditation.

Spiritually, meditation is instrumental in the meeting of human souls with the Universal Soul of God.

O God
Thy Presence is every where
Here and There
But no one Cares
To feel your Presence
To feel your Essence.

Some define you as Indefinable
Some others try to defy your Presence
In their Arrogance.

But O Power Great
Whenever I Meditate
My inner voice Tells
To search Myself
To feel your Presence.
To feel your Essence,

When we talk about visions, we realise that Meditation Power is the main reason for the happening of visions. Through Meditation, our brain knowingly or unknowingly attains the capacity to catch the happenings of future events at any universal frequency.

Can We See the Future Events

Some unknown power was showing me the future events through visions in early morning dreams. When I saw the first vision, I was very confused. I was not able to understand the impact of this vision. I was not aware whether this vision would be true or not. Truly speaking, I had no knowledge of such supernatural things. However, when this vision became a reality after some hours on the same day, then only I realised that it was a supernatural incident.

We come across many astrologers and saints who are able to predict future events. We know about Nostradamus, who predicted the future of countries many years before the happening of those incidents. Cheiro is also a well-known name who was able to see the future and make future predictions.

In India, astrology is considered a form of divine science based on the place of stars in the universe at the time of birth of a newborn. Astrologers prepare a full life chart by just knowing the exact time, place, and date of the birth of a person. Similarly, some persons are able to predict the future of a person based on palmistry.

It means the future is written beforehand. The question is, who writes the future and what is the basis of writing the future of a person? Our Hindu philosophy says that the destiny of a person is written based on the karmas of the person. Good fortune for good karmas, and misfortune for bad karmas.

As we sow, so we reap.

My Spirituality

Since childhood, I had a strong spiritual inclination. Born into an Arya Samaji family (a sect of Hindu Religion that does not have faith in idol worshipping), I never had faith in superstitions and was not very religious. I used to meditate occasionally during childhood but never entered into a real meditative form. After completing my Chartered Accountancy, I started a business and suffered huge losses. That period was the worst for me. I suffered financially, mentally, and physically.

During that period, I regularly did Pranayama (Breathing Exercise) and Meditation. Those days, I came across a book 'Autobiography of a Yogi' that changed my way of thinking. I realised that we are suffering due to 'Sanchit Karmas' (Stored past Karmas) of our past lives, and our present acts determine our future. As we sow, so we reap. I also joined Art of Living sessions of Sri Ravi Shankar to learn the process of 'Sudershan Kriya' (a form of Breathing Technique).

During that period, I had certain supernatural experiences, and I realised that everything is pre-destined, and destiny can be known or seen beforehand.

I experienced regular visions in those days. I saw visions in the early hours of the morning of someone dying, and every time someone close to me died within twelve hours of the vision. I also experienced some other supernatural occurrences that entirely changed my way of thinking towards whatever was happening around us.

I tried meditation on my Chakras and learnt Kriya yoga (a form of yoga to meditate).

I did not have any Guru, though I was searching for a Guru to guide me properly. One day, while in sleep, I went into deep meditation and felt myself outside my body, face to face with a bright light. I saw that I had come out of my body and was looking at my other body sitting in a lotus posture. I felt my other body experiencing explosions inside it. Later, I realised that it was Kundalini Awakening. This awakening experience changed my whole life.

For me, God is an all-prevailing supreme power which is present everywhere in some form of energy, and we call him Parmatma or God. That superpower is present in all living beings, also in the form of Atma or Soul. This is just like the water in the ocean and water in the pot; we can contact the superpower at any time provided that we know the proper method. This is as easy as switching on the light. There are many power points in our bodies called Chakras through which we can be connected with that Superpower Generator. We can ask for anything from that power, and we will get that, whether the requirement is material, physical, or spiritual.

Visions

An experience of seeing some future incidents in advance, in trance, dreams, or during meditation, is called a vision.

Many people experience these types of visions. Visions are mostly seen by saints and spiritual individuals, but sometimes, common people also have such experiences. Most common individuals are puzzled by these experiences and visions.

I started seeing visions when I was about 40 years old, and this continued for some period. I realised that the incidents which occur in the present time or in the future are predestined, and a superpower controls our whole life. It is commonly believed in India that the destiny is written at the time of birth, and it can be known by reading the birth charts by an astrologer.

A Great Super Power
Writes the destiny of us all

On the basis of our PAST KARMAS

In my case, I saw all visions at 4 am, which is Brahms Mahurat (time of God) as per Hindu philosophy.

It was just like a movie trailer for a few seconds, and the full movie was shown later. It was as if the trailer was broadcasted by God Channel and caught at a certain frequency by the brain, then shown to us immediately. The visions are always different from dreams; dreams are mostly vague and of long durations, but visions are specific and last only seconds. I always woke up after such visions, immediately checked the time on the wall clock, woke up my wife, and informed her about them. I never slept on those particular mornings when the visions occurred.

In many cases, some persons see such visions in trance or meditation also. They are even able to narrate such visions to persons around them. This is usually considered as the influence of some soul or ghost who controls their minds and makes them utter such visions, which usually come true.

Miracles

Bhagavad Gita

At that time, my son Vibhore was studying in 12th class, and as per the Student Exchange Programme of his school, two visiting students from Latvia were staying at our home as guests. They stayed with us for about seven days. I thought of gifting them two copies of the holy book Bhagavad Gita (holy Hindu book) but forgot to purchase the books until the last day the Latvian guests had to leave our home.

On the last day of their stay with us, I was sad for not purchasing the book. There was no book store near our residence, and the guests had to leave by the next morning.

In the evening, my wife Vandana asked me to accompany her up to the nearby temple. As we reached the temple, I saw two ladies from Iskon standing on the roadside and waving copies of Bhagavad Gita for sale. I was too happy to see them and purchased two copies of the Bhagavad Gita.

I gifted those copies of Bhagavad Gita to my guests. I had been living in that area for the last four years, and that was the first time I saw someone selling the Gita there. After that day, I never saw those women in our area.

Was it a coincidence or a miracle that on the same day I wished to gift those holy books to my guests, the Iskon members came there for selling those books, and that also at that particular time when we reached that place.

Rajiv Jayaswal
Author

Blessings of Lord Ganesh

Vinay Gupta is a businessperson and visits my office once a year to get his income tax returns filed. This year, when he visited my office, he was accompanied by a friend named Sudhir Panwar. He introduced himself as a police personnel attached to a Judge in a Delhi Court. While having tea, we started discussing spirituality and miracles in the lives of some people. I noticed that he got interested in our discussion about miracles. He told me that he had witnessed a miracle in his own life some years back. I asked him to narrate the incident, and below is the story of that miracle in his own words.

I belong to Baghpat District of Uttar Pradesh, and my village is Sunhera Village. I got a job in Delhi police in the year 2003 and shifted to the Shahdara area of Delhi. After office time, I used to visit a nearby temple and often gave donations to beggars sitting outside the temple. One day, an old beggar woman to whom I daily used to give some eatables asked me if something wrong was going to happen in my family in the village and that only Lord Ganesh could save us from that tragedy.

In my village, no one used to worship Ganesh during Ganesh Chaturthi days, but during those days in that year, I decided to bring an idol of Lord Ganesh to my village home and to do worshipping as per full customs. During those Puja days, when I was in my village home, my younger brother Ashok got high fever, and one day his condition deteriorated to such an extent that we had to carry him to our village doctor. On the way by car, when we were carrying him to the doctor's clinic, I felt that some unknown power was trying to protect him from the jaws of death. When we reached the clinic of the village doctor, he told us that there were only bleak chances of the survival of my brother and he should be immediately admitted to a big hospital. By that time, he had become fully unconscious, and his pulse rate was falling. We moved towards the city hospital carrying him in our car. He was lying in my lap inside the car. I had a strange feeling that some power was trying to save him from the clutches of death.

I started reciting the name of Lord Ganesh and was praying to him to save my brother. Then suddenly, a miracle happened, and the condition of my brother started improving. By the time we reached the hospital, he had become fully conscious. The doctor advised us to treat him at home for some days.

The miracle had happened, and my faith in Lord Ganesh had miraculously saved him from dying. Now, our whole village used to perform the Ganesh Puja with full rituals every year during Ganesh Chaturthi (a Hindu festival).

Sudhir Panwar
(Delhi)

Blessings of Father

Sometimes, such incidents happen in life that no one will believe except the person with whom they occur. Here, I would like to narrate one such incident that happened in my life. At that time, I was studying in the 12th class in Kanpur. My Father fell very ill during those days. He was very keen on marrying me into a good family, but destiny had other plans, and he passed away. After some years of his death, I got married. My husband was living in Lucknow at that time. Life was moving smoothly, and after some years, I became the mother of two boys. My husband got a job in Delhi, and I shifted to Delhi with my husband and sons, starting to live in a rented flat.

My father often used to come in my dreams, and I was a bit surprised by such dreams. One night, he again appeared in my dreams and told me that he had kept a fixed amount of money for me and had come to hand over that money to me. I also dreamt that he gave me a bundle of notes and told me that he would give me more of that money, specifying the amount. When I woke up, I was surprised and puzzled by this dream but ignored it, considering it simply a dream.

After some days, my husband decided to purchase a flat, and we chose a flat and gave some token money to the seller. I was stunned to note that the token amount given by my husband to the seller was the same as I had seen my father giving me in my dream. The total value of that flat was also the same as my father had promised me to pay in my dream.

I ignored all this as a coincidence. Finally, we purchased and shifted into that flat. One afternoon, someone knocked at the door of my flat.

When I opened the door, I saw a Sikh boy standing outside. He told me that he was selling nameplates for flats. I tried to avoid him, but he requested me to see a sample at least. Unwillingly, I asked him to show a sample nameplate. When he showed me one, I was stunned, and my whole body started trembling because the name written on that nameplate was Sardar Satbeer Singh, which was the name of my late father. That boy told me that his name was also Satbeer Singh. I got very emotional and called my husband there and told him everything.

He asked the boy to make a name plate for us. The boy made a nameplate for the flat and went away smiling after fixing it outside our flat gate.

After that incident, I often saw my father in my dreams, always asking me to call him to our residence. I talked to my brother over the phone and told him everything about my dreams and about that incident. He sent me a framed photo of my father, which I kept in our drawing room, and I felt that my father was showering his blessings upon us from that photograph.

Days were passing, and I was forgetting the above incidents as a coincidence when suddenly, once again, that Sikh boy visited my flat. He smiled and asked to clean the nameplate with a cleaning liquid. I remained standing there in surprise as he cleaned the nameplate and went away smiling, without charging anything. I stood there staring at him until he disappeared.

I came into the drawing room and looked towards the photograph of my father, feeling that he was smiling.

Gurvinder Kaur
(Ghaziabad)

Blessings of Guru Ji

Raj and Aashu Manchanda are our old friends, and we used to live together in the same society some years back. At that time, they were in great financial distress. They have two sons, and now both of them are married and well settled.

The Manchanda family says that their life changed miraculously after coming in contact with Guru Ji (a holy saint) through an acquaintance. Aashu Manchanda narrated to me her experiences of the holy miracles and blessings bestowed by Guru Ji:

We were in a bad phase of life, and I started selling life insurance plans to people to earn commission income. One day, I went to meet someone who was injured in an accident. He was a follower of Guru Ji and narrated his miracles to us, telling us that all our financial problems would be solved if we received the blessings of Guru Ji. We decided to visit the temple of Guru Ji in Chhatarpur, Delhi.

We went to meet Guru Ji at the Empire State and got mesmerised by his spiritual attraction. We decided to visit him regularly, but at that time, we were in great financial stress, and it was difficult for us to afford even the petrol required for our car. However, I was optimistic that we would face no problem due to the blessings of Guru Ji.

In addition, the miracles started happening in our lives. When we reached home after meeting Guru Ji, my younger son Rishab told me that he had received a call from a petrol pump stating that he had won some free petrol in a gift coupon. Initially, we ignored the call, but when we received another call, we decided to inquire about the gift. We were surprised to learn that, as per our gift coupon, we were entitled to receive 75 litres of free petrol in three instalments.

I realised that Guru Ji had solved our problem, and now we could visit him many times by our car. However, our financial conditions were improving by the blessings of Guru Ji, but still we did not have much money to spend for the better education of our children.

Risabh was willing to do a pilot course in Canada. It was very difficult to get a visa for Canada, and a lot of money was required for travel and expenses abroad. We decided to apply for a bank loan against the mortgage of our residential property, but our property was not legally registered. A neighbour offered to provide his property papers to secure the bank loan. While the bank loan was in process, that neighbour asked us to return his property papers as he had changed his mind. However, with the blessings of Guru Ji, we were able to secure the bank loan after registering our own property.

We had no support or acquaintance in Canada and were very worried about his stay at that place. However, blessings of Guru Ji were with us. One day when I was sitting in Satsang (holy congregation) of Guru Ji, I felt that Guru Ji was asking me to have no tension and telling me that one person named Bhatia would help us regarding his job as a pilot. Later, I came to know that one Mr. Niraj Bhatia, who was a follower of Guru Ji, was the owner of an Aviation Company named Summit Aviation and had also received divine instruction from Guru Ji to help Rishab. The pilot training of Rishab started in the year 2007. My husband and both sons had also become great followers of Guru Ji. We all were receiving guidance from Guru Ji in our visions. Many times, we were sensing fragrances of Guru Ji at our home, and many other miracles were happening in our lives.

My son, Rishab, faced many problems during his pilot training in Canada but was able to overcome all problems successfully due to the blessings of Guru Ji.

Guru Ji left his physical body on 31st May 2007, and we were badly shattered due to his departure, but Guru Ji came in our visions and assured us that his divine presence will always help and guide us.

Once, when we arranged a Satsang (religious congregation) of Guru Ji at home, Guru Ji asked us in a vision to renovate our home beautifully. We were puzzled as we did not have enough money for renovation, but we were able to do it with the blessings of Guru Ji, and a lotof devotees took Prasad (holy food) at our home Satsang.

Raj and Aashu Manchanda,
(Delhi)

God Saved My Father

At that time, we used to live in Shahdara at our ancestral home. It is a big home with commercial shops of brothers on the backside of the home.

That day, my father was sitting at my brother's shop, and it was time to close the shop.

He came out at the entrance of the home and asked the servant to shut down the shutter of the shop and lock it.

The worker was trying to lock, but due to some problem in the lock, he was not able to do it.

At that moment, my father, who was standing at the entrance gate of the home, rushed towards him.

As soon as he got down from the entrance and moved towards the shutter, the big marble slab above the entrance gate fell down.

He and the workers were stunned. If he had not moved from the entrance gate, the marble slab would have fallen on him.

God saved him miraculously.

Rajiv Jayaswal
Author

Lost Voice Recovered

Neeraj Sharma is my college friend. He is a media professional and was working with some TV channels earlier. He has also done Hindi dubbing for National Geographic Channel. He has been associated with All India Radio for 47 years. He has an A-Grade radio drama voice and still voices for radio and TV commercials.

During 1991, his wife lost her speech due to an injury as a suitcase fell on her head. Though she received treatment from many hospitals, nothing happened. Some doctors advised electric shocks, but the family refused.

One of his friends advised him to go to Ram Darbar Chandigarh, a place of Spiritual Sufism founded by Mata Rambai Ji Maharaja, known as Marie Kalandar Ammi Huzoor Shashanshah. At that time, she had already left her physical body, and her disciple, Baba Sakhi Chand Ji Maharaj, was the head of the temple.

Thursday is an auspicious day, and Pooja (Worship) is performed on that day. His maternal uncle, Shri Ram Joshi Ji, was in Chandigarh and was a devotee of Ram Darbar.

He took them to that Darbar. There they saw a lot of devotees sitting in front of him and telling him their problems. Finally, their turn came, and they requested him to cure the speech problem of his wife. Baba Ji asked his uncle to give him one cigarette, took a long puff, and put his hand on his wife's throat, declaring that everything would be all right by the grace of God. Baba Ji asked his wife about her problem, but she was not able to utter a single word. Then Baba Ji asked one of the disciples to give them pure water in a pitcher. He gave them five cardamoms from beneath his mattresses along with holy water and instructed them to take onedrop of holy water in the morning and evening, and two cardamoms in the morning and evening. Baba Ji then asked them to leave the room, have the kitchen langar of the Darbar, and instructed one of the disciples to give them buttermilk at the kitchen langar.

They reached Darbar Langar Hall for Langar (Meal). There were about twenty persons sitting in the hall for community Langar. When Langar was being served, suddenly he heard his wife saying that buttermilk should not be served to their younger daughter due to the winter season. He asked his wife in disbelief whether she had said something. She got up from her place, came near to him, and repeated her sentence that buttermilk should not be served to their daughter as it was very cold. He spoke loudly in disbelief and great pleasure - can you speak? Everybody in the hall was surprised and started raising slogans in praise of Ram Darbar and Baba Ji. They rushed towards the room of Baba Ji, but he did not allow them to enter his room and asked them to come to him again the next day. It was an unbelievable miracle.

This miracle motivated them to visit Ram Darbar often and become disciples of Ram Darbar. This was a great miracle, and afterwards, many other miracles happened in their lives.

He still remembers the wording of the first Qawwali (Spiritual Song) there:

> Kisi Ko Kuch Nahin Milta
> Teri Ata Ke Bagair
> Khuda, Bhi Kuch Nahin Deta
> Teri Raza Ke Bagair

(No one gets anything in this world without the grace of GOD.)

Baba Sakhi Chand Ji Maharaj gave his own voice to his wife, Mamta, as he had lost his voice two days earlier before leaving this world.

Really, GOD IS GREAT.

Neeraj Sharma
(Delhi)

Miraculous Escape

In our life, sometimes strange incidents happen, and we are left amazed to describe those incidents as miracles. I would like to narrate one such incident that happened to me, in which my life was saved miraculously.

On that night, at about 11:30 p.m., I was working with my laptop in my drawing room on a chair table in the middle of the room. Suddenly, my younger son, Vibhore, came to me and insisted on me giving him my laptop for some time. Although I was working, seeing his insistence, I agreed and left the place. He sat on the chair where I was sitting, but he slightly moved the chair back from its original position and started working on the laptop.

I had just moved a little distance from there when I heard a loud bang on my back side. As I moved back, I was stunned to see that the big chandelier hanging above him on the roof had fallen, and big glass and wooden pieces had scattered in the drawing room, except on the chair where my son Vibhore was sitting.

My whole family and some neighbours reached there and were stunned to see the scene. If Vibhore had not insisted on me leaving the place, the chandelier would have fallen on my head. I would not have survived or would have been seriously injured. If he had not moved the chair back, he would have been hit.

We all were surprised to see this miraculous escape. I still remember that incident many times and thank God for saving us.

Next day, I experienced my inner conversation with God. I thanked God with folded hands and tears in my eyes. I narrated this conversation in my poem **ISHWAR SE SAMWAD (CONVERSATION WITH GOD).**

Rajiv Jayaswal
Author

Motor Cycle

This incident is from 1994 when I was stationed at a cement factory in Rajban near Paunta Sahib in Himachal Pradesh. Working in the marketing division of the company, I had to visit many places in the state. Being young and energetic at that time, I preferred to travel on my Bullet motorcycle instead of using public transport. It was both enjoyable and part of my official duties. On that particular day, I had to travel to a nearby place called Vikas Nagar for an official tour, so I set off on my Bullet motorcycle. The weather was pleasant with a cold breeze blowing, and I was enjoying my ride.

The road was empty, and there was no traffic at all. I was about to reach my destination. There were mango trees on both sides of the road, and the atmosphere was full of fragrance due to the smell of ripe mangoes.

All of a sudden, I felt as if my motorcycle was flying in the air much above the road. Then suddenly, the motorcycle descended and fell flat on the road with me on it. Some labourers working in nearby fields ran towards me and helped me stand on my feet. Luckily, I had not suffered any major injury except a scratch on my left hand, which later proved to be a minor fracture. All that happened so instantly that I was unable to understand what had happened to me. After some time, when I looked around me, only then did I realise what had occurred.

Some people had tied a rope around two mango trees to fetch mangoes from these trees. The rope had fallen from their hands and hung on the road like a swing. The hanging rope had encircled my neck and the rear mirror on the handle of my motorcycle, causing the motorcycle to move high above the road as if performing a stunt in a circus. This could have resulted in a major tragedy, but it was averted by the grace of God, and I was safe, only suffering a minor injury.

I was safe, but my family was very disturbed. My father forbade me to drive the motorcycle in the future and asked me to purchase and drive a car only. It was not possible for me to disobey my father, and I decided to sell my favourite motorcycle with a heavy heart. I consider it a big miracle that I was saved that day even after this major incident.

Mukesh Kaushik,
(Delhi).

Narrow-Escape

I would like to share an incident from my life that was predicted by my late grandfather, Sri Pradyumn Narain Singh, a world-famous astrologer, nearly 26 years before it actually happened.

My grandfather predicted in 1990 that I would face a life-threatening incident in May 2016. The odds are high, but I would have a narrow escape on account of my good deeds towards less privileged members of society and the blessings of your parents.

I still get goosebumps as I share this because the prediction came true. I was the 15th survivor of eighteen when our steamer capsized in the Yamuna. The reason attributed later was overload. I, despite being a non-swimmer, survived, but the three casualties were swimmers. May their souls rest in peace?

I owe my second life to my good deeds and parents' blessings. Indeed, they can change your destiny. This news was also telecast on television channels.

Ritesh Singh
(Prayagraj-U.P.)

Prayer Granted

Raajeev Narula is one of my family friends. This narration, which I am writing, is from about 15 years ago. At that time, he and his wife, Imma Narula, were running a chain of play-way schools in Delhi under the name of Aadharsheela Schools. He is very religious and used to visit Jhandewalan Temple and Gurudwara Bangla Sahab daily.

Mr Narula has three children, one son, and two daughters. At that time, all were unmarried. He fixed the marriage of his eldest daughter, Vishwani Narula, in a rich and respectable family of Delhi.

Before marriage, the function of the ring ceremony was organised in a farmhouse. It was the rainy season, and that day it rained heavily, which ruined the whole function. Though the function took place, there was a big loss to the Narula family as the function was supposed to take place in the open space of the farmhouse, and a great amount was spent on decorations, etc.

After the function, when one day Mr. Narula and I were discussing that day's event, he told me an interesting incident which was nothing short of a miracle.

He told me the whole incident, as mentioned below:

The bride's side had organised a programme at a farmhouse in the open lawn. As the programme was about to start, dark clouds covered the sky, and the drizzle began. It seemed that heavy rain might occur, resulting in a significant loss for the bride's side.

I went to a secluded place and sat in meditation, praying to God to stop the rain that day and let it rain heavily on the next day's function, which I was organising. I prayed to Maa Bhagwati (Hindu Goddesses) that if it rained that day, I would never visit her temple in the future. Tears were rolling down my cheeks as I prayed continuously.

All of a sudden, the rain stopped, and the dark clouds disappeared, and the function was organised in a grand manner. The next day, during my function, it rained heavily, but I was happy because that was due to my prayer to Maa Bhagwati.

Raajeev Narula
(Delhi)

Saint Shri Madho Prasad Ji

It was September 1979 when my friend Shiv Harsh Tiwari asked me to accompany him to meet Saint Shri Madho Prasad Ji, a retired public prosecutor who lived with his wife and children. At that time, I had no faith in gurus or saints but just visited Madho Ji out of curiosity.

When I met him for the first time, he became very happy to see me. Later, he told me that he was my Guru in a previous birth and was waiting for my visit to him in this birth. At that time, I had joined my job in ARTO some months back. I decided to ask him a question about my transfer from this city to another city in the near future, as I knew that transfers do not take place in a short span.

Guru Ji stared at me and replied that my transfer order had been dispatched, and I would receive it by next Sunday. This prediction was a big surprise for me, as I had no inkling about any such transfer order.

He also told me that my wife was pregnant, and there were chances of abortion. I was stunned as only my wife and I had knowledge of her pregnancy, and we had not told anyone about it.

Next Sunday, DM met me on my way to the office and informed me about my transfer to another city. On the same day, my wife had an abortion and remained in the hospital for one month. I went to meet him again and requested him to advise me on how to stop my transfer. He suggested I contact my father-in-law (who was an IAS) and ask him to assist me in halting the transfer. Following his advice, my father-in-law successfully managed to stop my transfer order.

Once he told my wife and me about our previous births. He told me that in previous births, he was a Saint in Rajasthan, and my wife and I had come to meet him when his followers looted and killed us. He told us that he was waiting for us in this birth so that he could give Diksha to us. He initiated us as his disciples (Diksha) on Basant Panchami Day.

On 21st January 1980, we went with him to attend the marriage of my niece at Balia (in U.P. state) by road. During our journey, he told us that a Saint was ailing near the riverside, and he had to cure him. He cured him by giving medicine to him.

When we reached my brother's place, we found out that he was in great pain due to piles, and it was not possible for him to perform kanyadan (daughter's marriage rituals). Guru Ji cured my brother of that disease by giving him some herbal medicines, and he was completely cured.

He performed a miracle at the time of the marriage ceremony when heavy rain started pouring just before the marriage time, and he stopped the rain by performing a Hawan (fire worship ritual) at that place, and we were able to perform the marriage ceremony.

Once Guru Ji went on a pilgrimage to Maihar Devi (near Prayagraj) with us. On our way back, we visited the family of my maternal grandparents, which was nearby. Their family members asked him many questions about the future, and all his replies proved true later on. One of my relatives asked him about the future of her daughter, who was only five years old at that time.

He replied that she would have an inter-caste love marriage, and it proved true when she became young. They asked one question about her brother as well, and he said that he would have an injury in his eyes. No one believed him at that time, but all his future predictions proved true in the future.

Guru Ji never used to disclose his supernatural powers to outsiders, and only a few of his disciples knew about his spiritual powers. Even now, many years after his death, he guides me whenever I come across any problem.

We often used to ask him many questions, and his answers always proved true. Once, when the famous actor Amitabh Bachhan was badly injured during a film shooting fighting scene and was hospitalised in a very serious condition, we asked Guru Ji about him. He replied that the actor would be perfectly cured after some time, and the same thing happened.

Once, my friend Shiv Harsh Tiwari asked him about the future of the then Prime Minister, Indira Gandhi. He replied that Indira Gandhi would face no danger in the whole world, except in her own residence. This proved true when she was shot dead by her own security guards at her residence.

T.N. Singh (Retd. IAS)
(Lucknow)

Stolen Scooter Recovered

This incident is of fifty years back when I was very young and used to live in Mansarovar Park, Shahdara with my parents. That was a period of rationing and permits. There used to be very few two-wheelers on roads during those days. Having a scooter at that time was a privilege. One had to do advance booking and a long wait before finally getting a scooter. My father, Mr. Ramesh Kaushik, was working in a government office and was entitled to a quota for scooter booking to get priority in getting the scooter. Finally, he managed to get a scooter in the government quota by paying his lifelong savings in government service. I still remember that it was a Vespa scooter of yellow colour. We used to keep that scooter with great care inside a room in which we used to sleep. We were afraid that this scooter should not be stolen in any case. At that time, I was just ten years old. We children were supposed to do cleaning of that scooter every day. Particularly on Sunday, we used to wash and polish the scooter. Helping our father in getting the scooter inside and outside our residence by pushing it was also a part of our duty. Waiting to hear the sound of the scooter horn in the evening was also a part of our daily routine.

Days were passing smoothly, but one evening there was a knock at our house gate instead of the usual honking of the scooter horn. There we saw our father standing at the gate, but our scooter was nowhere to be found. Our father's face was pale and he looked very tired. He entered the home and sat inside the room. When my mother asked him about the scooter, he did not respond. When she repeated her question, he replied that his scooter had been stolen. At first, we thought he was joking, but seeing his expressions, we realised he was serious. That night, none of us was able to sleep. The next morning, my father left for his office on foot, and going by public transport became his daily routine. A police report was made for the theft, but nothing happened. I still remember the news published in a local newspaper about the scooter theft. Days passed, but there was no news of the scooter. For some days, an atmosphere of gloom prevailed in our residence.

With every passing day, the atmosphere of home became normal. We were trying to come out of our gloom. One evening, when we, family members, were relaxing at home, the doorbell rang. When we opened the door, we found a man of about 30 years standing at the gate. He asked whether it was the residence of Ramesh Kaushik. When we confirmed, he asked to talk to him. We asked him to come inside. He entered and started talking to my father in a whispering voice. All family members became curious about what he was saying. We all stood around them and tried to listen to their conversation. We were surprised to hear what he was telling my father. He confessed that he was the person who had stolen my father's scooter. He also revealed that the stolen scooter had been recovered by the police and was in the custody of the local SHO, who had not even documented the recovery in the police records and was using the scooter as his own.

We all were very surprised. We offered him tea and asked him to elaborate on the whole matter. He repeated that the scooter was in the illegal custody of the local SHO, and we could recover it from there. He told us that he had obtained our address from the scooter documents kept in the scooter dickey.

Next day, my father went to that SHO who flatly refused that the scooter had been recovered and was in his custody. Having no other option, my father went to meet his superior. He welcomed him as he knew him personally and had respect for him as a poet. My father narrated the whole incident to him. He called the concerned SHO and asked him to hand over that scooter to my father. He had no other option but to obey him, and he gave us the possession of our scooter.

We all were overwhelmed with joy. Our precious scooter was again with us. It was really a miracle that the thief himself had come to our home for confession and informed us that the custodian of law had become a part of his crime in a strange manner.

Strange are the ways of God.

Mukesh Kaushik
(Noida)

Sai Miracles

Faith & Patience

I got married on 31ˢᵗ January 1989. By the grace of Sai Baba, I am blessed with a loving family.

I conceived three months after getting married. My elder sister-in-law and younger sister also conceived at the same time.

Days were passing happily. Everyone in our family was taking care of us.

After three and a half months of conceiving, I had a throat infection and high fever. My husband and I went to a gynaecologist, and she prescribed a few medicines. But that night, I felt really uneasy and was not feeling well. The next morning, my husband took me to the clinic again, and the doctor suggested we go for an ultrasound.

After the ultrasound, the doctor told us that the baby died inside the womb. This statement shook us to the core. It was a moment of disbelief. It literally made me feel like me, my sister, and my sister-in-law were ready for a race, and I fell down flat on my face. It is a feeling that cannot be expressed in words. However, as loving and caring my husband and my in-laws are, I soon recovered.

One day, my sister-in-law took me to a Palmist or "Jyotishi" who was well known for his correct predictions. He told me so many correct things about my past after reading my hand. Therefore, my sister-in-law asked him about any predictions regarding my child, to which he told us very firmly that I do not have any line for a child and there is no hope in the future as well. Those words shattered me, and I was in great pain. I waited every month for good news only to receive none.

One day, my husband planned to visit Shirdi with our family members. We attended the "Sai Mangal Snaan" (Holy Bath) and the "Kakad Arti" (Morning Prayer) with full faith. After that, two years passed, and I had still not conceived, even though the doctors we were consulting had run many check-ups on me and my husband, and there was nothing to worry about at all. These things reminded me of the predictions of the "Astrologer" and worried me.

After a few days, my husband took me to a famous Sai Baba temple in Lodhi Garden, Delhi, and I prayed to my Sai Baba to bless me with a child.

As the Vachan says:

"Man mein rakhna, dridh vishwas. Kare samaadhi, puri aas."

"Aa sahayata lo bharpoor, jo manga vena hi hai dur."

To my greatest surprise, I conceived the next month.

Doctors, Check-ups, Predictions by the Astrologer, everything seemed insignificant in front of the faith that I have in my Sai Baba.

Shradha and Saburi, these two virtues, made me overcome the biggest worry of my life.

Today, I am a mother of two. My son is an IPS officer, and my daughter works in one of the top MNCs as a Software Engineer.

Moreover, I tell them this and many other stories of Sai Baba's miracle.

Seema Chhabra
(Delhi)

Lost and Found

On that day, while coming to the office by my car, I put my briefcase on the back seat of my car. My office was about four kilometres from my residence. On the way to the office, I stopped my car at a petrol pump to fill the fuel. After filling the fuel, when I came out from the petrol pump, I noticed some currency notes in front of my car. I stopped the car and came out. Some passersby also reached there and told me to hand over the notes to the petrol pump employees so that if anyone came there to claim the money, they could hand over those notes to him. I handed over all the money, which was in the form of ten-rupee notes and was not more than three hundred, to the petrol pump employee.

I started my car and parked it outside my office. After reaching the office, I asked my peon to bring my briefcase from the car.

He came back and said that there was no briefcase in my car. I was stunned. Where had my briefcase gone? Suddenly, I remembered the currency notes episode outside the petrol pump and realised that I had been conned by some conmen. They had stolen the briefcase from my car by involving me in the currency notes. I got worried. That was the income tax period, and my suitcase contained various tax and personal records of my clients, which would be very difficult to replace.

I went again to that petrol pump and inquired about my briefcase and the identities of those conmen, but got no clue from the petrol pump employees. I called the police and made a complaint about this theft.

I searched all the nearby places but did not find my briefcase. I was worried as the last date of income tax returns was very near, and all the relevant documents of clients were in that briefcase.

About five to six hours had passed, and I had no hope of finding the briefcase. I prayed to God to help me. Suddenly, I got a call from the nearby police station, and the police inspector asked me to reach a nearby mall. As I reached there, I saw a big crowd along with some police officers. The conmen had left my briefcase there as they found no cash inside.

I was happy to find all the documents intact inside the briefcase, except for a big photograph of Shirdi Sai Baba (a Holy Saint) that was kept in the briefcase.

Had Shirdi Sai Baba helped me in locating my lost briefcase, it was really a sort of miracle for me.

Rajiv Jayaswal
Author

The Rickshaw Puller

I work as a social science teacher, and the incident that I am sharing today is from the time when my school examinations were taking place. One day after school, I was heading home with my daughter, Nimisha, who was studying in 1st standard in the same school, and one of my colleagues, Mrs. Meena. I was carrying a blue cotton bag containing two examination answer sheet bundles of my class, and we were waiting for our regular rickshaw-puller.

As we were waiting for a long time and he had not come, we thought of taking another rickshaw. As we all sat in the rickshaw, I kept my blue bag under the seat and got involved in the regular chit-chat. While talking to Mrs. Meena, I noticed that the rickshaw puller was wearing a very neat and clean-ironed pistachio-coloured shirt. As it is my favourite colour, it caught my eye.

Once we reached our destination, Nimisha asked if we could have some pastry from the nearby pastry shop. I asked her to select the pastry she wanted, meanwhile, I paid the rickshaw puller, and Mrs. Meena went to her house, which was nearby.

In a blink of time, I realised that the blue bag containing the answer sheets was not with me. I immediately asked Nimisha about it, and she did not have it either. Furthermore, in moments, I realised that I had left the bag in the rickshaw.

Oh my God! I screamed as the rickshaw puller had gone by then, and I could see him fading away at the corner of the road. Nimisha ran after the rickshaw. I told her to stop him. I was worried about her as well, as she was too young and for the first time alone on the road. I called Mrs. Meena as well, and she consoled me.

I started chanting "Om Sai Ram" as I was worried about my daughter, but thank God, she came back. She was very exhausted and told me in a very low tone that she could not catch the rickshaw.

That is when Mrs Meena suggested that we should go back near the school, as the rickshaw puller belonged to that area and might go back there.

We went back near the school and started to search for the rickshaw. I started to chant "Om Sai Ram" repeatedly and prayed to Baba to send the rickshaw puller. I was so worried about the repercussions and what actions the school might take against me. They could have given me a memorandum, or they could have fired me. How could I be this irresponsible! I felt so helpless. As there was no way I could have found that rickshaw puller out of hundreds of them when I did not even remember his face. The only thing I remembered about the rickshaw puller was his pista coloured shirt. However, I had full faith in my Sai Baba. I gave all my worries to him and started to chant "Om Sai Ram".

As He says:

"Bhaar tumhara mujh par hoga, Vachan na mera jhuta hoga" (I promise you that your burden will be on me).

Suddenly, on the other side of the road, I saw that pistachio-coloured shirt and in a split second recognised it. I immediately started calling to him from the opposite side of the road, and then he noticed us and stopped the rickshaw. I ran to the rickshaw and saw my blue bag tied to it.

He told me that he went to his house for lunch and took the bag inside. His two kids, who were studying in a government school, informed him about the importance of the examination answer sheets, and he was coming back to the school to return the papers.

I took a sigh of relief as I held my bag in my hands and thanked my Baba a hundred times.

Seema Chhabra
(Delhi)

My Visit to Shirdi

At the beginning of that year, I received many New Year Greeting Cards with a picture of a Saint. I inquired about him and discovered that he was known as Shirdi Sai Baba, an ascetic Saint who used to live in Shirdi, Maharashtra. Many people in and outside India worship him and have witnessed his miracles. However, he passed away many years ago, yet many still claim to witness his miracles. I also experienced one such miracle.

On that day, while returning home from the office, my car stopped at a red light. When the green light occurred, I tried to start my car, but it did not. I tried again and again, and when it did not start, I came out of the car and tried to push it, but it did not move. Many other vehicles were behind my car, and they were getting restless. I again entered the car and tried to start it, but all in vain. Tired, I sat silently on the seat, prayed to Shirdi Sai Baba to help me, and closed my eyes for some moments.

A person knocked at my car window and asked me if I needed help, and told me that Shirdi Sai Baba had sent him to help me. I could not believe my ears for only some seconds before I had prayed to Sai Baba for help.

I came out of the car. He sat in my seat, and to my surprise, the car started immediately. The man came out of the car, and after thanking him, I inquired about his identity. He told me that he lived nearby and was passing by when he saw that my car was not starting. Sai Baba had asked him to help me. He also gave me Holy Ashes of Sai Baba and moved from that place.

The whole incident was unbelievable and felt like a dream. I reached home and told my wife about the entire incident. She was also very surprised and told me that Sai Baba himself had come to help me.

I had never been to Shirdi. The next day, I booked a ticket for Manmad, the station for reaching Shirdi.

As I reached Manmad, I enquired my co-passengers about reaching Shirdi. One of them asked me to accompany him up to Shirdi in his car. He took me up to Shirdi with him, provided me breakfast at his residence, and arranged a hotel room for me.

Incidentally, he was a member of the Shirdi Temple Trust, which allowed me to enter the temple through a VIP door. I was able to pay my respects to Shirdi Sai very comfortably.

This was truly a miracle in my life.

Rajiv Jayaswal
Author

Super Natural

A Soul Trying to Indicate His Presence

FIRST INCIDENT

It appears that the untimely death of a family member, or his attachment with the family members, stops a soul from moving out from that environment, and sometimes the souls give some indications to show their presence there.

It is very painful for a family to lose any member of the family. During the corona pandemic, I lost my husband. There were only three members in our family, and after the death of my husband, only my daughter and I remained. It was very difficult for us to come out of the loving memories, and often I saw him in my dreams.

I live in a society Flat in Ghaziabad. This incident is of 28 December 2021. I got up in the morning and was preparing the school tiffin for my daughter. When I came into the drawing room to pick up her school bag, which was kept on the table, I suddenly saw fingerprints of a hand on the outside of my drawing room window. I was surprised to see those fingerprints as my flat is on the sixth floor, and it is nearly impossible for anyone to leave their fingerprints from outside. I called my daughter, Kuhu, and showed her those fingerprints. She was also surprised. There were clear and visible handprints on the outer side of the window. Both of us were very scared to see those handprints as it was not possible for a human being to make them from outside, as there was no base to stand on outside our sixth-floor flat window.

I told Kuhu that these handprints were of her father, whose soul was nearby and was trying to indicate his presence to us.

SECOND INCIDENT

On that day, I was alone in my flat. All of a sudden, strong winds started blowing, and I tried to close all the windows and doors of the flat. As I entered the kitchen to close the kitchen window, the kitchen door slammed shut due to a strong gust of wind. There was no handle on the inner side of that door. I tried to open that door, but it was closed so tight that I was not able to open it. I tried my best to open it, but all in vain. As I was alone in the flat and there was no one to help me, even my mobile phone was in the drawing room.

My daughter Kuhu had gone to school, and it was time for her to come back, but there was no one to open the door for her as I was locked in the kitchen. I was panicked and started weeping, remembering my husband who had passed away some months ago. I started talking to him in my thoughts that due to his untimely death, I was facing so many problems, and if he were alive now, he would have opened the door by pushing it from outside. All of a sudden, I felt as if someone had pushed the door from outside, and it opened. I was surprised as there was no one outside, and it was not possible for me to open that door from inside.

I came out from the kitchen and found that my mobile phone was ringing. It was my daughter on the other side of the phone asking me why I had not picked up the call, as she had been trying to contact me over the phone for the last half an hour. I told her about the entire incident, and she was also surprised. She said that the soul of her father had helped me at that time.

Once again, the soul of my husband had indicated that he was present with us.

THIRD INCIDENT

That was the month of June, and the temperature was touching 45 degrees. On that day, it was noontime, and all the doors and windows of the flat were closed. I was sitting on my bed, engrossed in the memories of my late husband, and weeping. Suddenly, I felt a cool breeze around me. I was surprised as to where that cool breeze had originated since the room AC and fan were closed, and it was not possible to feel such a cool breeze during the noontime of a very hot day. I realised that the soul of my husband was around me, trying to indicate his presence to assure me that he was there to help me.

Raama Singh
(Kaushambi, Ghaziabad, U.P.)

A Spiritual Doctor

At that time, I had started a Slimming Centre in Delhi. The Centre was on the first floor, and the landlord, Mr. Gupta, used to run a property dealing business on the ground floor of the building. We used to sit and talk occasionally. There was a doctor's clinic nearby. The doctor was very religious, and the walls of his clinic were adorned with pictures of Hindu Gods. His residence was about five kilometres from his clinic, and he used to walk to his residence on foot instead of hiring an auto or taking the bus. Once when I asked him the reason, he told me that he walked on foot so that he could get more time to recite the name of God while walking.

One day, Mr. Gupta and I were sitting and having spiritual talks. I told him a story about the meaning of life. The moment I finished the story, the doctor entered the room and sat with us. He told us that he wished to narrate a story about the meaning of life and started narrating the story from where my story had finished. Mr. Gupta and I were astonished and started looking at each other in surprise. We were surprised at how the doctor was able to know the story I was narrating, or was it simply a coincidence that he started narrating the next part of the same story. There was no way he could have known what we were talking about inside the room.

Whenever I think of that incident, it surprises me.

Rajiv Jayaswal
Author

A Stranded Traveller

To take rest and respite from my busy life, I often set out to the hills in my favourite Thaar jeep along with my wife, Vishuma. Let me tell you about her. She is an adventurous biker, trekker, and an ardent rover. Both of us together travelled thousands of miles in dangerously difficult terrains, jungles, and hills.

It is not long when I planned a dangerously difficult about 1500 km long trip to Leh. I set out along with Vishuma in my jeep. The weather was inclement. I was passing through Shingla Pass in Himachal Pradesh at a height of about 16500 feet. It was terribly raining and snowing. It was frightening to see hundreds of feet deep gulch on the roadside. Visibility was quite poor. To take rest after a long drive and to get relief from backache, I parked the jeep on the roadside and got down. I took a deep breath to get over the boredom and to freshen up my mood. I could hardly set myself right; the hills around me appeared to be spinning. At high altitudes, the mind gets confused because of the lack of oxygen, and the vision becomes erratic. All of a sudden, I heard a feeble voice. Initially, I thought it might be due to a confused mind and lack of oxygen. I was stunned when a formidable image, totally drenched in mud, appeared crawling out of the JCB Machine parked on the roadside and moving towards me. It made me cry with fear. Was it a ghost in the wilderness? After seeing it with attention, everything became clear. In fact, it was a man crying again and again for help in his feeble voice. He was perhaps injured and sick and not in a position to walk. Not far away on the JCB, a helmet was visible. I was stunned to listen to what he told me in his broken Hindi. In fact, he was a South

Indian youth having a passion for long-distance travelling. A day back, his motorbike slid on the ice on the road and fell into a 50 feet deep ditch. Somehow, he mustered courage and reached the road. Since a day back from 3 PM, he was lying under the JCB without food and water in bone-chilling cold weather, heavy rains, and snow. He was injured and had a high temperature. Under such precarious conditions, he could not survive without immediate medical aid. We wanted to help him, but our jeep was fully packed with luggage and hardly had any space to accommodate him. We immediately pitched our tent and shifted him there to provide protection from rains and snow.

Unfortunately, this was not the normal route and did not have enough traffic. We took it by mistake at the tri-junction. Therefore, we turned our jeep back in search of help. After travelling for a short distance, we sighted an Endware car from Delhi. Two young boys were sitting in the car. We narrated the whole story to them, and they immediately agreed to help. Not far away, some Border Road Organisation employees were sighted. They also agreed to help.

All of us then reached the spot and shifted the injured into the vehicle. Now, we were in search of a hospital. After travelling for about an hour, we sighted Jipsa – Gaimur Health Centre. It was located about 50 feet down the road and could be approached through a staircase. We carried the injured on our backs, but the Health Centre was locked. We succeeded in finding the healthcare staff. The injured received first aid, and we were advised to shift the injured to Kelong District Hospital.

We shifted the injured to the vehicle and then proceeded to Kelong District Hospital. It was about 20 km away. Here, there was also a shortage of staff, so we had to shift the injured ourselves on the stretcher. We could not trace the contact details of the injured's family. He was now in safe hands and did not require our presence. Therefore, we set out on our journey. We kept track of the well-being of the injured. After 15 days, he was discharged. During the treatment period, BRO helped him immensely.

The incident had an effect on our minds, and we considerably changed our plan of travel. In fact, what one proposes does not always happen. Is it not strange that we undertook the wrong route and got stranded? Possibly, some unknown power influenced our decision and made us turn to the wrong side to help the south Indian youth in danger. Whether we believe it or not, His ways are strange.

Mohit Tiwari

Conversation During Meditation

This incident was narrated to me many years ago by the late Ms Prem Lata Mehta. She was a senior Bank Officer with Punjab National Bank and was a Spiritual Personality. She was also the sister-in-law of my best friend, Virendra Chhabra. She used to meditate daily for many hours.

At that time, she was working as a Manager with the PNB, Preet Vihar Branch. She had very cordial relations with all the Bank Staff except one lady who was a clerk in that branch. That lady was in the habit of disobeying the instructions of Ms. Mehta. She always tried to harass her in one way or another. She even used to spread false rumours about Ms. Mehta in the branch and to the customers. Ms. Mehta was very disturbed due to her nature. She tried to talk to her many times to understand the reason for her annoying behaviour, but that lady never opened her mind.

Ms Mehta used to get up early every morning and was in the habit of meditating. One morning, while in meditation, she focused her concentration on that lady and talked to her. During meditation, she conveyed her mental message that she was never against her and was pained by her unruly behaviour. She also conveyed the message that she had forgiven her for all her faults.

That day, when she reached her bank and settled in her cabin, that lady entered and started weeping while touching her feet. Ms. Mehta was surprised by her actions. She asked her to calm down and explain the reasons for her distress. Ms. Mehta was astonished to hear the explanation given by the lady. She recounted that in the early morning of that day, she had seen Ms. Mehta in a dream who had a conversation with her. The lady was repeating the exact conversation that Ms. Mehta had messaged her during her meditation. From that day on, the lady's behaviour towards Ms. Mehta changed completely, and they developed a very cordial relationship.

This was really a miracle.

Late Prem Lata Mehta
(Delhi)

Encounter With a Soul

I have witnessed many miracles in my life, but this one was different. It was not a vision or intuition, but an encounter with a soul.

Our CA firm was allocated the audits of Tehri Hydro Company. The company was constructing a dam on the Tehri River. Every year, we had to go to Rishikesh for the audit purpose, where we used to stay in the guesthouse of Tehri Hydro. The guesthouse was on the bank of the River Ganga, and the surroundings were very panoramic.

I was in the habit of having a long walk in the evening. That day, I went out for a walk near that guesthouse on the bank of the river Ganga. After some time, I realised that I had come very far and that was an isolated place. I decided to go back towards the guesthouse. Suddenly, I saw a figure coming towards me from a distance. I noticed that something was strange with the movement of that figure. She appeared to be an old woman. When she reached near me, I was stunned to notice that her way of walking was amazing, as if her feet were not touching the ground. My whole body was trembling with fear. When she came closer to me and I saw her face, I was unable to believe my eyes. It was the face of my grandmother who had died about ten years back at that time. She was staring at me and walked away.

For some time, I was not even able to move. I was feeling as if I was seeing a dream. Had I encountered a soul? How could my grandmother, who had died many years back, come again to meet me? My grandmother used to love me very much, and I was much pampered by her during my childhood. Was it her love for me that forced her to meet me again even after her death?

Whenever I think about that incident, I get puzzled.

Rajiv Jayaswal
Author

Maze of Lines on Palm and God's Will

I very often think whether the lines on the palm have any effect on our fate. Can we predict our future by reading these lines? There is a volley of such questions that flash in my mind. I am of the opinion that this is sheer a matter of your faith like idol worshipping, i.e., if you have faith the idol is God in the guise of stone, otherwise merely a piece of stone. In fact, our faith also changes with time and circumstances. Despite being a staunch atheist, one remembers God at the time of tragedy. As far as I am concerned, I all along had faith in God and at the time of tragedy, my faith in the Almighty surges immensely, giving me enormous strength to face the situation. A tragic incident that I am going to narrate happened to me in difficult times in 2003.

In 2003, the company in which I was working had a great financial crunch. Employees did not get salaries for months. Even the existence of the company was at stake. It was not sure whether the company would survive or be locked down. Employees were facing a very difficult time. In such a crisis, the company announced a Voluntary Retirement Scheme (VRS). Employees were in great tension. I was also bewildered about my future, not knowing what to do. Incidentally, somebody advised me to contact the famous astrologer Pandit Badoni Ji residing in the nearby town Vikas Nagar. As I was in tension and not finding any way to face the situation, I decided to contact Badoni Ji. Without losing any time, I visited Badoni Ji along with my wife Neeta. He patiently listened to my problems and after thoroughly studying my palm lines, he told me, "Your services in the company will continue."

He also alerted me to drive the vehicle cautiously, lest I should collide with the footpath.

His prediction about the continuation of my services in the company gave me great relief, but his caution about the likely vehicle accident worried me. To ward off the likely accident, he advised me to wear a ring studded with a particular gemstone. The ring was available with Pandit Ji for £1200 to £1500. However, this was quite a sum in those days of financial hardship.

Neeta also understood well and, seeing me in dilemma, whispered to buy it from Delhi at a cheaper price. Neeta's suggestion was right in the present circumstances; somehow, I did not like it. I said, "In such matters, one should not try to save money." Doubting her faith in palmistry, I told her, "One should either have full faith or no faith in such matters." Sensing my mood, Neeta agreed to buy the ring from Pandit Ji. Despite her repeated persuasions, I stubbornly refused to buy it, telling her that now we will buy it from Delhi only. Perhaps this was God's will.

I very well remember it was 23rd March 2003. After some time, as per our plan, I left Rajban (Himachal Pradesh) for Delhi in our car, Maruti 800, along with Neeta and daughter Shreya. In the pleasant weather, we were enjoying the ride. The car was running at a normal speed of 70–80 km per hour.

We were just passing through Murthal (Sonipat). Suddenly, a speeding car was found coming from the wrong opposite direction. In order to avoid a collision, I turned my steering to the right, resulting in hitting the road divider at full speed. The car lost its balance and rebounded on the road 3/4 times. My head hit the car roof and got injured. I lost consciousness. Neeta's foot was injured. The car windowpane was broken, resulting in throwing Shreya outside. She was lying on the road with her broken thighbone, crying with unbearable pain. You can make out what a formidable scene it would have been! By coincidence, because of the India – Australia Cricket World Cup Final match, the traffic on the Chandigarh - Delhi road was not heavy. This saved Shreya from any other likely tragedy. Because of the accident, the car doors got jammed. Some people working on the roadside took me out forcibly. I was still in an unconscious condition. After some time, the police and a PCR van also reached the accident spot. We were all admitted to the Murthal Primary Health Centre. My family members in Delhi were informed. They reached Murthal and got us discharged after first aid; we were then taken to Delhi. I was admitted to Chandiram Hospital in Delhi. The hospital at that time discharged me after some treatment. However, later I had to undergo complex brain surgery at Sir Gangaram Hospital in Delhi. Shreya and Neeta also had to bear the ordeal for a long time because of the injuries.

Today, all of us are happy and healthy, by God's grace. Our lives were saved. It is now like a sordid dream in our minds.

About Pandit Ji's first prediction, even after 20 years, I am still serving the same company, whereas the majority of my colleagues left on VRS in 2003.

When I look back, I firmly believe that God endowed me with new life by protecting me and my family from a disastrous accident. This is MY VERY FAITH.

Brij Mahana
(Delhi)

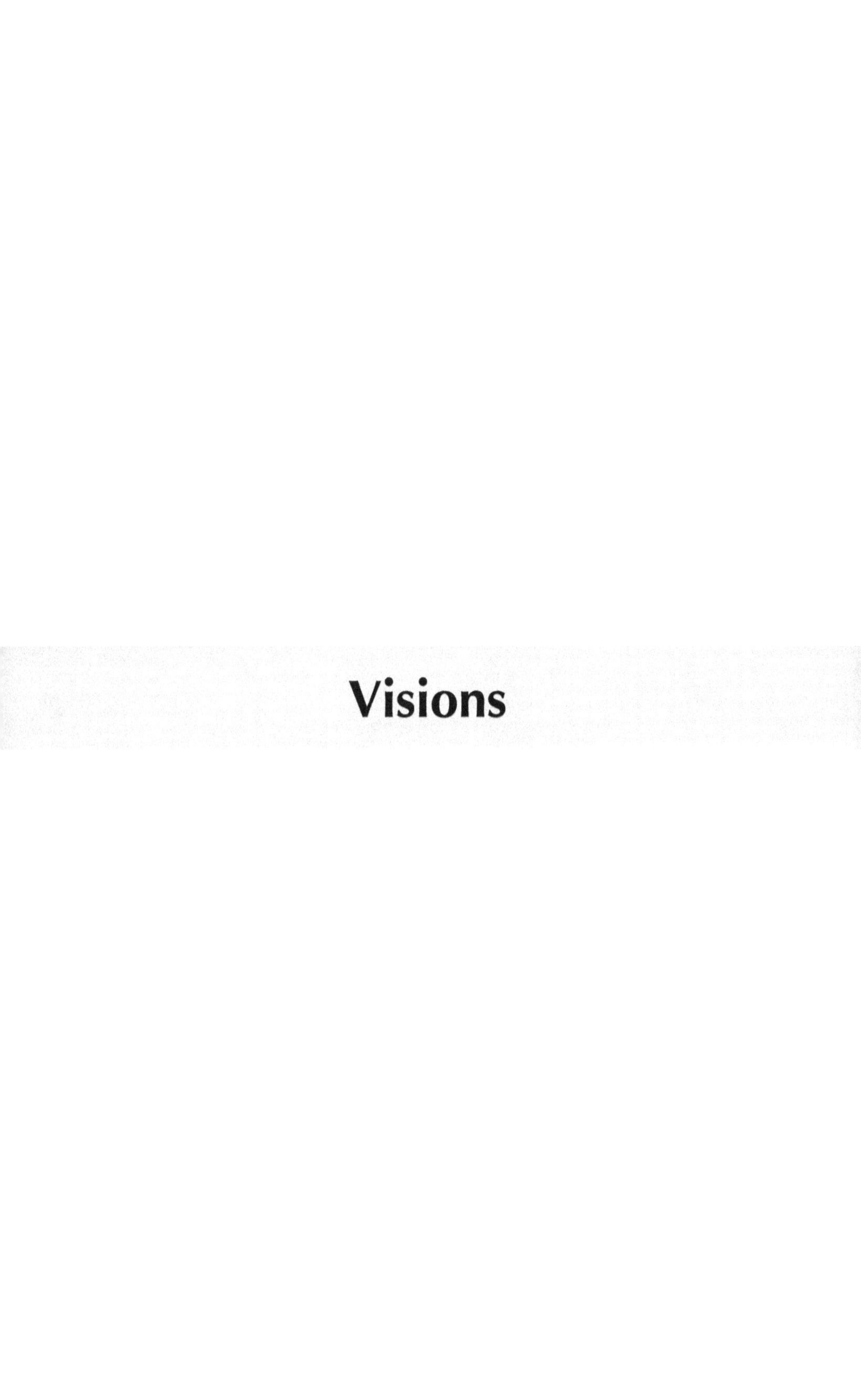

Visions

Car Accident

This incident is from Ambikapur (Chhattisgarh) during the month of November 1990. I was studying in the 12th class at that time. I was an ardent worshipper of Lord Shiva. On that night, I had a dream at 3:00 A.M. that my younger brother was driving a car on a winding road when suddenly the car fell into the valley. I saw the car upside down, and the wheels of the car were spinning in the air. I woke up startled, my heart filled with apprehension of a possible untoward incident. I felt it was a bad omen and that something bad might happen. I started praying to God. On the third day, the doorbell of my home rang at 3:00 A.M. I was praying at that time, hoping that no untoward incident would occur.

We opened the door and found my brother-in-law with one of his friends. They had come to us at that odd time to inform us that my brother was hospitalised due to a car accident. During that time, there were no mobile phones, so he had personally come to inform us about this incident. There was chaos at home, and everybody became panicky. We got ready and left for the hospital. The place where the accident took place was on the way to the hospital. The car was still visible in the valley. Moreover, I was surprised to see that I had seen the same scene I had dreamt three days back. Later, we came to know that there were some other persons also in the car at the time of the accident. However, luckily, no one had died, and all were able to come out with the help of some local villagers, who helped them in hospitalisation. I felt that sometimes some unknown power gives us the message of future happenings.

Klein Jaiswal Rai
(Madhya Pradesh)

Glimpse of Swami Vivekananda

At that time, I was living in Bathla society at I P Extension. I witnessed most of the miracles of my life at this flat. One morning, I also witnessed a strange vision during meditation.

I saw a glimpse of Swami Vivekananda in front of me, which disappeared within seconds. I got out of meditation. I had a strange feeling. There was a strange aroma in the room. I thought I had seen a dream while meditating.

I came out of my meditation room. It was about 4:00 in the evening. As I entered my drawing room, I saw an invitation card lying on the table. When I saw that card, I was stunned. There was a photograph of Swami Vivekananda on the card. The invitation was for Vivekananda Jayanti (Swami Vivekananda's Birthday).

I inquired from my son about that card, who informed me that one Mr. Hegde from our society had come to invite me for the function, while I was in meditation, and surprisingly, I had seen the glimpse of Swami Ji at the same time.

Mr. Hegde was my neighbour and the chief manager of Vijaya Bank. He was a member of Ram Krishna Mission and a spiritual person.

I immediately went to the flat of Mr. Hegde to meet him and found him at his residence. He welcomed me and asked if I had received the invitation card. I told him about the glimpse of Swami Vivekanand in my meditation when he had come to my residence. He was very surprised and asked me how Swami Ji looked. I explained to him what I had seen. He was even more surprised. He took me to another room where there was a calendar of Swami Ji on the wall. To my utmost surprise, the calendar photo was the same as what I had seen in my meditation.

I still cannot believe that I had seen Swami Ji in my meditation.

Rajiv Jayaswal
Author

Healer

Ashok Kumar Sharma was the President of Veer Puru Society, Rohini, and I was the auditor of that society. The office bearers of that society often used to come to my office for finalisations of their financial statements. Ashok Sharma was an aged man. I always found something strange in him. His aura was very positive. He also had expertise in curing bone problems, cervical problems, and nerve diseases.

One day, as he was sitting with me, I asked him about his expertise, and he narrated an interesting story of his life.

He told me that he was having a daughter who one night got up and told that she had seen Maa Vaishno Devi in her dreams, and she was asking her to visit Vaishno Devi Temple. As their family was a God-fearing family, they planned to visit Vaishno Devi Temple.

As they were walking on the mountain road towards Vaishno Devi, the landslide started, and big stones began falling from the mountains. All the pilgrims, including his family, started running to safe places. Unfortunately, one stone fell on his daughter, and she died immediately.

This was a big tragedy for their family. They came back to their residence. The tragedy was chasing their family. After some time, Ashok Sharma was diagnosed with a brain tumour. He was operated on for the tumour but was not cured and remained bedridden in a serious condition. One night, in desperation, he prayed to God that either he should be cured or should die. Suddenly, he saw a vision in which someone informed him that he would be completely cured by the next morning and would be blessed with the power of curing muscular, bones, and nerve diseases at a particular time in the morning.

He was astonished to see this vision and discussed it with his family members. All members were astonished, and they asked him to test his power.

Next morning, he called some patients suffering from bones and nerve problems. He felt as if someone inside him was guiding him to cure the patients. The patients were fully cured. Since then, he started this process of curing such patients daily in the morning from 10.30 to 3.30 noon, and by the grace of God, he was able to cure all. Surprisingly, he does not feel any hunger for food also.

Later, he got associated with ISKON and changed his name from Ashok Sharma to Amrit Krishna Dass.

I was surprised to hear his story. God had gifted him miraculous power after great tragedies he faced.

Ashok Kumar Sharma,
(Delhi)

Miraculous Recovery

Nobody knows what will happen in the future. The future is uncertain. But many times, we come across some indications of future happenings in advance. Here, I would like to narrate one such incident.

Mr N. K. Agarwal is my friend and is a practicing chartered accountant in Delhi. He told me an incident that happened with his wife. His wife had gone into a state of depression. She was very disturbed, as if she wanted to say something but was not able to. All family members were worried about her condition.

All of a sudden, her younger son, who was 12 years old, got ill. Despite the doctor's treatment, his condition deteriorated, and he had to be admitted to the hospital. There was a lack of water in the child's body. The doctor informed his parents about his critical situation and admitted him to the ICU. One day, the child's condition became very serious, and it seemed like he was not going to survive. All family members were worried.

The doctor tried his best, and the child's condition started to improve. After some time, he came out from that critical situation and was discharged from the hospital. When the child came back safely home, Mrs. Agarwal also emerged from her depression.

After narrating all this, Mr. Agarwal remained silent for some time. I asked him how all these things were related to the depression of Mrs. Agarwal.

He informed me that Mrs. Agarwal was continuously seeing a dream in which she was witnessing the near death of her child. She could not tell all this to anyone, and she was going into depression.

It was an indication of a future happening regarding her child's health condition. Mrs. Agarwal was foreseeing the future illness and the near-future death condition of her son in her dreams regularly in advance.

Rajiv Jayaswal
Author

Visions of Death

The School Teacher

My children used to study at a Reputed International School in Delhi, and I was the Secretary of the Parents Teachers Association. There was also a Teachers Association in the school, and Rashmi Chugh was the President of the Teachers Association. We, as members of the PTA, often interacted with members of the Teachers Association in meetings, and Rashmi always gave intelligent suggestions regarding the betterment of the school.

Once, the Teachers' Association went on strike against the school authorities to pressure them for their demands, and they asked for our support. During their strike, I often used to interact with Rashmi, and we became good friends. After some days, their strike ended.

During those days, I was witnessing strange visions during early morning time, which always happened to be true. One such incident happened that morning also. Last night, I had a telephonic conversation with Rashmi, and we talked for about an hour and had planned to meet soon to discuss some important matters. Next morning, I suddenly got up after a strange vision in which I saw a young girl entering a room, lying down on the floor, and covering her body fully with a white sheet. I saw myself entering that room and asking that girl to get up and to uncover her face. I saw that girl flying in the air and disappearing in the air.

I got up, my whole body was shivering. I woke up my wife, Vandana, who was always a witness to my visions. I was aware that my vision would come true the same day and someone is going to die that day, but I was not aware of who he or she would be.

I became restless throughout the day, and the day passed. In the evening, I got a telephonic call from a teacher of the school who told me that Rashmi had died due to a sudden heart attack. I was stunned. I had talked to her last night for about an hour, and we had planned to meet within two to three days.

I reached the residence of Rashmi. Her body was lying on the floor, fully covered with a white sheet. My vision had come true; I had seen exactly the same scene in my early morning vision. I had already seen the vision of her death many hours before.

Rajiv Jayaswal
Author

A Lady in Ambulance

The Bose family were my next-door neighbours. They were very nice people and were very close to us. Mrs. Bose and my wife, Vandana, used to interact with each other daily.

Those days, some guests from Punjab had come to meet them and were staying with them for a few days. One early morning, my doorbell rang. When I opened the door, I found Mr. Bose standing there. He asked me to give him my car keys as my car was parked behind his guests' car. I said that I would move my car myself, but he insisted on having my car keys, mentioning that their guests were in a hurry. I was a bit surprised by his behaviour, but I handed him my car keys.

The same morning, I had seen a strange vision at exactly 4:00 AM. I saw a female dead body being carried away in an ambulance, and people talking about the death of that lady. My wife, Vandana, was the witness of this incident as well, as I had told her about my early morning vision. I had remained disturbed throughout the day. I was aware that something tragic was going to happen but was not aware of what that tragedy was.

The day passed without any untoward incident, and I reached home. When I entered home, I saw Mrs. Bose talking to my wife. She looked very disturbed. My wife told me that the car of their guests was crushed by a truck, and one of their female relatives had died.

My early morning vision had become true. I had seen a female being carried away in an ambulance, and her relatives talking about her death.

Strange are the ways of God. No one knows about the identity of that writer who writes the destiny of all of us.

Rajiv Jayaswal
Author

A White Figure

Is life predestined? Who is that great writer who writes our destiny? No one knows about him. Can we get intuition or vision about the incoming death of someone?

During that period, I was getting regular visions about incoming deaths, but those visions never disclosed the identity of the person who was going to die. This case is also of such incoming future death prediction. I always got such visions at 4:00 A.M., which is called Brahma Mahurat (the time of God).

I saw a white figure entering our society through the main entry gate. The figure was human-shaped and was flying in the air. It came up to my residence and moved towards the back side of my flat. I tried to follow it, but suddenly my uncle, who had died many years back, appeared before me and forbade me from following that figure.

I got up, my whole body was shivering. I saw the time; it was exactly 4:00 A.M. I immediately realised that I had just seen a vision and some tragedy is going to happen that day. I woke my wife up and told her about this strange vision. Both of us were sure about the happening of a tragedy. The strange thing was that although destiny had disclosed a future tragedy to me, it had not given me any power to avert that tragedy.

The whole day, I remained disturbed. I was praying to God that nothing bad should occur. I reached my house in the evening. I had just finished my dinner, and then I got a call from our neighbour that one Mr. Bansal, who used to live at the backside of my residence, had expired.

Now, I understood the meaning of the Vision. I had seen in the early hours of that day. I had seen the messenger of death entering my society and flying towards the residence of Mr. Bansal.

I was regularly seeing such types of visions in those days, indicating future tragedies, and all such visions used to appear exactly at 4:00 A.M. Strange are the ways of God; the more we try to understand them, the more we get confused.

Rajiv Jayaswal
Author

Breaking the Bangles

I saw a healthy, unconscious man dying in my arms, a weeping woman breaking her bangles. With a jerk, I got up. I had just seen a Vision of Death. Someone was going to die, but who? I was not aware of it. I woke up my wife, Vandana, and told her about this vision. She was aware of all my visions. We were not able to sleep that morning after that vision.

At that time, I was living in Group Housing society in Delhi. This was a society, consisting of various blocks of different-sized flats. I was in the managing committee of the society. During the summer season, there happened to be water scarcity in certain blocks of the society, and altercations among residents were very common.

We called a meeting of some residents from various blocks in the society office to resolve this issue. We were discussing amicably many problems faced by the residents. There were about ten people in that meeting. Suddenly, an argument broke out between Mr. Giri and Mr. Chawla, who were also members of the committee. They started shouting at each other, and we tried to pacify them. However, they continued shouting at each other for some time, and finally, we were able to restore peace.

Mr Chawla left the room and sat in an adjacent room, and we continued our discussion regarding other society matters. Suddenly, we heard strange voices coming out of the other room. We all reached there and found that Mr Chawla was having an asthmatic attack and was having trouble breathing. We informed his family members, and his wife reached there immediately. His condition was worsening, so we decided to take him to the nearby hospital by my car, which was standing outside the society office.

He sat in the front seat of the car beside the driver's seat, while his wife and a Mr. Srivastava sat in the back. I drove towards the hospital. Mr. Chawla's condition was worsening. Suddenly, he became unconscious and collapsed onto me. With great difficulty, I managed to drive, and we reached the hospital. I got out, and we tried to help him out of the car, but he fell into my arms. The doctor arrived and declared him dead. His wife started weeping and breaking her bangles.

Suddenly, I remembered the vision I had seen in the morning. A healthy man lying in my arms and a woman weeping and breaking her bangles. Nature had informed me in advance about the future death of someone, the identity of whom was disclosed then. I was stunned.

Is life predestined, and are all the incidents pre-planned?

Rajiv Jayaswal
Author

Deepika

Deepika is a simple lady with no spiritual background. She has faced many adversities in her life. Her husband died at a young age, leaving her and two small daughters behind. After his death, she was in great depression and did not used to sleep at night. Suddenly, she felt that something was happening inside her. She started feeling vibrations in her Chakras. Sometimes, she used to feel that her soul was floating outside her body. She also started getting visions of the future. Here, she has narrated certain future visions seen by her—

1. I used to visit the home of one of my family friends. There, I came across the daughter of her sister who was having a problem with water retention in the upper part of her head. Doctors had fitted a tube in her head so that such water could be extracted from that portion. The small girl was in much pain and distress. I used to feel pity for her. One night, I saw a vision of a garlanded photo of that girl. When she woke up, she felt that something very bad was going to happen to the small girl. After three days, when I visited the residence of my friend, I came to know that the diseased girl had passed away three days ago, exactly at the time when I saw that vision. I also saw her photo with garlands hanging on a wall there. My vision had come true.

2. I was a member of a ladies' kitty party some years back. Once in that party, I noticed a kitty member sitting behind me with a big bindi on her forehead. Suddenly, I realised that the bindi had disappeared. After some moments, I saw the bindi had reappeared on her forehead. A strange feeling came over me that something bad was going to happen to her.

After one month, when I visited to join the next month Kitty, I did not find that lady at the kitty party. When I inquired about her, I came to know that the husband of that lady had died. I was surprised that my strange feeling about that lady had come true.

Deepika Gupta
(Delhi)

Terrific Dream

It was March 2000. My father was admitted to the ICU, Nephrology department, Lucknow PGIMS. He was on CAPD after his renal failure, for the last 10 months. He was battling between life and death.

In the midnight of 10th and 11th March, probably, I saw a terrific dream. I saw that I am travelling on Ram Nagar Bridge, Varanasi, over Ganga River, with many of our family members in a car. I was wearing a black printed cotton suit which I had at that time. In between, I saw a number of people, a kind of mess around, somewhere in a place, which was not known to me.

In another part of the dream, I saw myself wearing a green chicken work suit and, in one of our courtyards, watering with palms in the south direction. It's a kind of Hindu ritual in which palms filled with water and sesame seeds are delivered respectfully in the south direction to our people who are in the heavenly abode. This ritual is done from the day of death until the 10th day. It was very hard to accept, but I had received a supernatural notification that very soon a death of someone close to me is going to happen.

On 14th March 2000, Tuesday, early in the morning around 5:00 A.M., I dreamt again and saw the temple near my home. It is a Lord Shiva temple with a Shiva Lingam in between and Shiva family idols just around the Shiva Lingam. I dreamt that all idols were scattered and broken. I almost screamed and woke up. Around 7:00 A.M., there was a phone call from Varanasi. My uncle called and told me that papa was no more.

All the relatives and people around started gathering at home. As per my father's last wish, the cremation was to be done at Manikarnika Ghat in Varanasi, a holy Hindu town.

In a hurry, my younger sister-in-law packed my bag. And we left for Varanasi by car. Upon reaching Varanasi, while travelling through the Ram Nagar bridge, a route we never used to take when travelling from Ambikapur, I was shocked to see that I was wearing the same black printed cotton suit that I had seen in my dream.

There, we came to know that the cremation had been delayed. Therefore, we had to reach home where they had kept my father's body. Finally, after midnight, he was taken to Manikarnika Ghat for cremation. When we reached home, it was sunset time, and everyone hurried for the palm water rituals as I have discussed earlier.

I was astonished to note that my sister-in-law had kept that same green chicken suit in the bag for me to wear for performing the rituals, which I had already witnessed in my dream.

Klein Jaiswal Rai
(Madhya Pradesh)